# J O Y   D U S T

## ILONA AT 96

First Printing: 2016
ISBN 978-0-692-78367-2
© 2016 John Mark Lucas
John Lucas/Fourth Chakra House
PO Box 25231
Winston-Salem, NC 27114
info@ilonaat96.com

www.ilonaat96.com

Ordering Information:
*Joy Dust, Ilona at 96* is available online at www.ilonaat96.com

Special discounts are available on quantity purchases by corporations, associations, educators, and others.
For details: orders@ilonaat96.com

For my loving special friends.

Ilona

# J O Y  D U S T

## ILONA AT 96

by ILONA ROYCE SMITHKIN

AND JOHN LUCAS

Fourth Chakra House

I am now 96 years old.
As I sit alone in my studio, I chuckle to myself.
Ha! I'm still here!

I am an artist.
And lately, I'm even a little bit of a celebrity.
I find that funny. But I also love it.
I love it because now, young people come to me to look for
answers to their problems.
They think I am wise.

I don't know about wise, but I do feel I am down to earth and that
I am pretty logical.
And I think if you are lucky enough to live a long life,
you should share what you've learned.

I have learned a lot.
I look back on my life now without regret
or a wish to change anything.
All I want is to understand.
Is that wisdom?

I am positive and optimistic.
But, like everyone, I too have my dark moments.
The tough times usually have to do with my body.
Aging takes its toll on a body.
That's an understatement.

So when the storm clouds roll in, what do I do?
I lift my spirits by my bootstraps
and write about my feelings.
The writing helps me understand the ups and downs of life.
I just put it all on paper,
and then I know what I'm dealing with.

In this book, I'm going to share with you some of the intimate and
personal discoveries I've come to understand.
At 96 years old.

*I hope you read this with a smile.*

For over 40 years,
I've spent my summers in Provincetown, Massachusetts.
It's at the very end of Cape Cod.
It's magic.
Full of artists and life.

Some days I am overwhelmed by the joy of being alive.
Here to see the sea, the waves, the sand, and in the distance the
boats, the lighthouse and the harbor.

The next moment I fall into a deep sorrow,
knowing I have to leave soon.
That's when I take a pen and write down my thoughts,
or draw or paint.

*You must smell a flower when it blooms.*

Often when I walk on the street,
my knees stiffen up and they lose all flexibility.
I feel like I would like to lubricate them with a can of oil.

I want someone to invent a garment, like a beautiful corset.
Something that is fashionable.
But instead of lifting my bosom,
it will lift each leg as I take a step.
What a wonderful invention that would be.

*Never forget that even a small step can be a step forward.*

A new understanding or discovery occurred to me this morning.
I was anxious and rushing to do something in my apartment,
and I almost stumbled.

I stopped to think of the concept of "Impatience."
What does an extra moment matter?
What *would* matter is if I fall and hurt myself.
That would take much longer to fix.

I thought how each part of us has a solid foundation.
All the various parts of our body make a team.
So I started communicating with each part of my body.
My toes...
My feet...
My knees...
My stomach...
My shoulders...

I feel that my head holds all the necessary knowledge,
to protect and advise.
Direct and command.

Everyone has impatience and is almost a slave to it.
We rush into an action as if we'll miss something important,
even if it is not.
We feel our time is limited, as if it is a rope pulling us.

*Stop rushing. Stop pushing.*
*Stop wasting your precious minutes by speeding.*

What a strange combination –
I look around my room and see warm reminders
of the "Now" and the "Past."

My work.
My paintings.
My clothes and costumes.
And the colors.

My mind combines all this and everything comes to life.
A mad swirl and it's all playful,
with the complementary accessories,
like creating a painting.

*Everything is creative. But you must see it or find it.*

Speed is a power all by itself.
It is self-centered.

Speed does not give you the benefit of observing
or taking in an experience.
Before you can enjoy a moment,
it is like the wind – gone.

It leaves all emotion behind.
It is all movement and blur.

*How will you create a memory,*
*if you don't see the moment you are in?*

My head feels stuffy.
My neck aches.

But I am very grateful that I can still walk.
Though with a wobble.

I hold on to anything near and solid.
My new dance partners.

*When the old steps do not work, you learn a new way to dance.*

Today I set myself several tasks.
One was to vacuum my rug.

But I came about impatience again,
and I stopped to think, "How driven we are."
I took a moment to write my thoughts on impatience.

What difference does it make if I clean now or later?
What is more of a priority,
to explore an important feeling or to clean house?

My thoughts are fleeting and may never return.
But my apartment will not change one iota,
whether the dust goes now or later.

*Don't miss the "joy dust" because of the floor dust.*

When we get old, people often want us to move...
...to a more protected environment
...to a warmer climate
...to an unfamiliar place

What they don't take in to account,
is that the older person is used to their environment...
...the chair, the bed, the position of the room.
There is a certain comfort in that knowledge.
If one uproots them they feel lost and separated
from their familiarity of space.

I feel it is easier to live in a crowded, small room.
Even with some inconveniences,
rather than to move into a new place.
Even if it is more functional.

I make do with what is known and familiar.
It gives me a sense of orientation and a feeling of belonging.

*If it ain't broke, don't fix it.*

The sun comes out after two days of grey and rain.
I open the glass door to my deck.

It is a little cool,
and I smile at the enchanting view.

The bay, water, boats; the stream following its direction.
Waves busy in steady movement.

Here is an eternity of peace, quiet and comfort.
My needs are met.

*Nature is always a perfect host. Learn to be a grateful guest.*

I contemplate my status.
Do I feel happy to be alone?
Yes, but in a way I never considered.

If I am with someone who is heavy,
in an emotional way,
then I almost have to carry that person.

It can become, like a burden.
Almost as if their presence is an imposition.
And talking to them to discuss it or clear it up is not possible.
They would not take it as an observation to ease the situation,
but as a criticism.

*Do you know why angels can fly?*
*Because they take themselves lightly.*

Old fashioned ways,
versus the new inventions.

Is it really progress?

With all the innovations,
are we living more peacefully?

With all the super communications,
are we more content or happy?

*Consider the heart and its needs.*

When I have an interview, of which there are many now,
the young interviewer usually asks a question of comparison.

Then or now?
Which is better?

How can I answer that?
Since everything has many answers.
Then and now have to be viewed separately.
With their own lens.

How can I say,
what I prefer is something long ago?
When my vision of things has broadened, has changed.
As well as my acceptance, through understanding and experience.

*The past has been difficult.*
*The present is good.*
*Because I have learned how to deal with it.*

When I was in the hospital,
I was stripped of any authority.
I was dependent on food servers, doctors, nurses.
Completely dependent on strangers.
Feeling rather helpless.

Now I'm at home.
Old and with a few limits.
But I can still move about.
Get things and watch the outside.

To be fully helpless is a great burden to yourself.
So every day and every hour is a constant struggle
to keep going and continue to do for myself.

*I may be the tortoise now, as my hare days are over.*
*But the tortoise still gets there, even slowly.*

Now everyone has to do bathroom functions.
So if one feels one has to go,
and one sits there yet nothing happens, one thinks,
"What a waste of time." (No pun intended!)

Not so.

Your friend and colleague —
the stomach and conducting systems —
are just not ready.
But they are steadily working on it.
They just need more time.
So talk to them, encourage them to do what is necessary.

*Your body works hard for you.*
*Make friends with every task you do.*

In daily life we have the same problems and worries
as in the old times.
How to make a living.
How to find love.
How to find who we really are and what we really need.

Today, I know every life question has several answers.
Not just one, as I believed when I was young.

Any happiness or problem is full of degrees.
Very few things are simple or have a clear answer.
Nothing is just black and white.

*The more you know,*
*the less one can make absolute statements.*

I have to lie down for a few minutes.
The words *rest in peace*,
make sense to me now.

It's just a quick nod, which powers me back up.

*Take naps now.*
*Even a few minutes, it will refresh you.*

I have a gift to give...
From me to you...
Learn this: *make do.*

We cannot rely on friends or family to help us with small things.
They have their own lives to live.
To make a living, to pay rent, electric, food.

How can I take that away from them?

So I make the most of what I have at my disposal as long as I can.
If it is truly urgent, I may ask for help, but only then.

People nowadays are spoiled.
They have most things handed to them.
Or they call for help when something doesn't work
or goes on the blink.
They are angry, lost and helpless.
They throw things away.

We, from the old world, have learned to be resourceful.
And we make do.
We leave things out or go without.
Or we invent new ideas or fix things to last temporarily.
Anything to help out and fix the problem.
We used to say, "Fix it with spit and glue!"

*I have a gift to give...*
*From me to you...*
*Learn this: make do.*

In the opera Tosca, in the last act,
the tenor sings before his execution...
"Never have I loved life more than now."

This is what I feel as I take my coffee
to the deck to taste the morning.
I look to the sky and I think,
"Maybe this is why I lived so long.
To experience and fully appreciate nature."

Where else could I see and feel and smell
the sky, sea, sand?

And most of all this quiet.
So potent.
So patient.

*Being alive means experiencing the recognition of all elements.*

When you get older,
you have to establish a very good relationship with yourself
based on discipline and trust and willingness to accept.

It is a time for seduction.
When I don't want to get up out of bed,
I postpone, a little more.
My other half, The Director, tells me…
"You have a lovely warm bath waiting,
with good smelling bubbles."

After my bath, I have a great comforting cream for my skin.
Then a little rest.
And then exercise.

After that, my special demitasse cafe, to get going.
And breakfast with goodies.
Two different cheeses, apricot jam, vases with flowers.
Then telephone calls to favored friends to remind them
they are great and remembered by me lovingly.
Then rest.

Later, I must seduce myself again to take my daily walk.
Up and down three flights of stairs.
I think of them as gym exercise.
And my nature walk, where I reflect on sand and sea and life.
Often I have resistance.
It is so much easier to stay put in a comfortable chair,
or to lie down.
But I make the effort to put one foot in front of the other.

What used to be so simple is now a project,
to be planned and executed.
Each project takes coaxing,
and convincing and seducing with care.

*You must be the caretaker to yourself. The protector and advisor.*

When I walk on the street or go up and down
my three flights of steps,
I go slowly.

Step by step,
holding on to the rail so as not to fall.

I think sadly that every child can run and go quickly,
and here I am, an old person.

Then I switch my thoughts to music.
And I sing in my mind the Toreador Song from Carmen,
"Auf in den Kampf Torero."

I have to laugh.
And the same steps, they are lighter, easier to go up.
Anytime I have a heavy, searing situation,
I remind myself to lighten up.

*I imagine I am a ballerina.*

I look out at the sea.
The waves are steady and an even flow keeps on coming.

I think of being positive and seeing situations clearly.
And yet, I also feel a lost soul somehow.
Where is the tower of strength or the consort battleship?

My body is getting weaker, but my mind is going full speed.
Constantly thinking, trying to find a solution,
being creative or solving a problem.

I am happy to have a free day with no obligations.
Today is mine.
I am lucky and humble to have this beautiful view of eternity.

*The tide of constant life and movement keeps me going.*

Sometimes when life seems too heavy or difficult,
I think of the time eight years ago.
I could not walk to the bathroom or kitchen.
Every part of my body hurt terribly.

So great was my pain, without relief,
that I did not want to live.

I was desperate to not fall into despair.
So I asked myself,
"How can I harvest something positive from all this?"
I picked up my pen
and started my *Pain Portraits*.
One drawing for each day I was suffering.
I drew 51 portraits before the pain suddenly vanished.

*I made pain the subject, instead of me being pain's subject.*

I look out from my deck
and the endless horizon is there for me to see and feel.

The air envelopes me.
The water is almost still.
The tide is out here and there.
Further on, some ripples.
Some boats leaning over, gently rolling, quiet.

I treasure the peace I have here.
The quiet, which once frightened me as being alone,
is now precious.

*I drink it all in. Thirsty to hold on as long as I can.*

What no young person realizes,
is the complete change of priorities and thinking as you get old.

Whether you like it or not,
your body becomes your focused concern.
Because you depend on it.

Some mornings, I wake up not wanting to move or get out of bed.
But I make myself do it.
Then I do my exercises,
the ones I've done since I had my hip replaced at 84.
I take my bath and luxuriate in it.

*Get up. Exercise a little. And plan your day.*

I have become aware of every little action or movement I make.
Every step is a production.
As is every decision.

When brewing in the coffee pot,
pouring the water into the pot is a problem.
I no longer have the strength to lift the full pot of water
and pour it into the maker.
So I take a small glass and pour the water
three times into the opening.

I work extra slow.
So I don't push against a hard surface.
My skin is so thin it breaks at the smallest bump.

When I eat I am very careful and conscious.
How I bite into bread or a roll, so as not to hurt my teeth.
Any damage would mean a long, tedious trip to the dentist.
In midtown.

*My body is old, but at this age,*
*it has earned all the love and care I can give it.*

This is an old story that always cheers me…

A man has a cat he loves.
But every night the cat consorted,
and a lot of noise came from the backyard.

The neighbors, being annoyed,
asked him to do something about this.
So the man took his tomcat to be neutered.

A week passed and all was quiet.
Then the noise started all over again.

The man took his cat inside and asked him,
"What is it with you? I went through a lot of trouble
and money to have you fixed. What is going on?"
The cat calmly said, "I don't do nothing boss. I sit on the fence
and I am a consultant."

*Experience is both a gift and a responsibility. You can share it.*

Today is a sunny morning and the tide is out.
I used to rush out to catch the view
from far out on the sand.
But now I have to consider my strength.
I am the caretaker of my body, the protector of my heart.

Every few minutes I have to lie down to rest.
I feel as if I have a child to protect and supervise.

I cannot make decisions or appointments
without consulting myself on my energy level.
I don't go to many parties or gatherings
because of my limited strength.

When I explain that to younger people,
their understanding can be limited.
They want their energy to be mine.

*Age is a valuable jewel that you must constantly polish.*

I was asked to speak to the crowd at an
*Advanced Style* book signing.
I had no idea what to say.
But I remembered how many people had come to me and said,
"You are an inspiration. I want to be like you when I get older."

So this is what I told everyone in the room:

*I want to give you a gift.*
*Every one of you.*
*When you get home tonight, look in your mirror.*
*Don't think of cosmetics or colors or fashion.*
*Just take a good look at your eyes.*
*How wonderful that they can see and explore things.*
*Then look at your nose.*
*How fabulous that it breaths, smells, sneezes and discovers odors.*
*Your ears, they hear and interpret meaning and discoveries.*
*Then move to your mouth.*
*It speaks and eats and drinks.*
*It can even kiss!*
*What wonderful miracles you possess.*
*Be grateful for these gifts.*

*Look for good.  Inhale deeply.  Listen for those you can help.*
*And speak with kindness.*

A heartfelt *thank you* to the photographers who allowed us to use their work in this book.

Front Cover: Frank Mullaney

Page 2: Ari Seth Cohen

Page 5: Elisa Goodkind, Co-founder of StyleLikeU.com

Page 7: Margo Isadora

Page 9: Ari Seth Cohen

Page 11: John Lucas

Page 13: Frank Mullaney

Page 15: John Lucas

Page 17: Ari Seth Cohen

Page 21: Robert Payes/Stiff Shots Photography

Page 25: Ari Seth Cohen

Page 27: Tom Cathey

Page 29: Mariateresa dell'Aquila, for Feminine Weapon Day 2015

Back Cover: Mariateresa dell'Aquila for Feminine Weapon Day 2015

Made in the USA
Middletown, DE
03 October 2021

49549305R00024